I0485442

A Note to Customer Service Managers:

Customer service professionals serve as the face of every company. They are often the only person the customer will ever interact with and the only impression the customer will get of the business. Given the importance of customer service, it is vital that representatives be given the training they need and deserve. This book is designed to give simple suggestions that customer service professionals can implement to make huge improvements in the service they provide. Allow your customer service professionals time to let these tips sink in. Continue to talk about these tactics and encourage a dialogue between the members of your department. When you show your team that you value amazing service and are willing to invest in it, your customer service professionals will follow suit!

As always, I am happy to address any specific questions. Feel free to reach out to me at **jh_solutions@yahoo.com**.

A Note to Customer Service Professionals:

For some people providing amazing customer service comes naturally. For others it takes some practice and hard work. Whether you are a natural or not, everyone can take their customer service to the next level.

Learning how to give amazing customer service doesn't need to be difficult! This book examines top-notch customer service and shows you 52 small things that can make a huge difference. Tackle one concept per week and improve your customer service without ever feeling overwhelmed!

Start with one concept and make that your focus for a week. The following week focus on another concept, all the while incorporating what you learned in the previous weeks. Week after week you will learn valuable skills to set your customer service apart from the rest. Customers will respond to your professionalism and enthusiasm, and you may even find your job gets easier as you get better at it!

Look for this icon throughout the book to learn phrases and words to use as you improve your customer service.

1) Master Your Greeting

Your company may have a preferred greeting that all of its employees are required to use. If there is not a predefined greeting that you have been instructed to use (or you are tasked with coming up with one) consider developing one yourself and sticking to it. Using the same greeting will help you become more comfortable and confident with it. If you have trouble remembering it, write it down. When you use the same greeting over and over again it will begin to sound more natural, and you will be less likely to mess it up.

Whatever that greeting is, make sure you greet the customer enthusiastically and with a smile in your voice. The customer will be able to tell if your heart is not in it. Chances are you have had interactions with other customer service professionals where they sounded half asleep, bored, or unhappy to be answering the phone. This immediately puts customers off and starts the conversation on a negative note.

Take a quick deep breath before you pick up the phone. This will give you a fresh perspective before helping the next customer. You only get one chance to make a positive first impression!

2) Thank the Customer For Calling

It is important that you thank every customer for calling. Most people do not enjoy having to contact customer service; they probably have other things they would rather be doing. Thanking them acknowledges they are taking time out of their day to contact you.

Thanking the customer for calling can be done at a few points during the conversation. This can be part of your greeting.

- *"Thank you for calling XYZ Company. This is Claire. How may I help you?"*

- *"Thanks for calling. This is Amanda. How may I assist you today?"*

It can also be done after the customer tells you the reason for their call.

- *"I appreciate you calling. I'd be happy to help you with that."*

- *"Thank you for calling to let me know. I'd be glad to resolve that problem for you."*

The end of a call is also a good opportunity to thank the customer for calling. You can build this into the closing (ending) of the call.

- *"Thank you for calling. Have a great day!"*

- *"Thank you for calling us today. Please let me know if there is anything else I can do for you."*

- *"We appreciate your call. I look forward to working with you in the future!"*

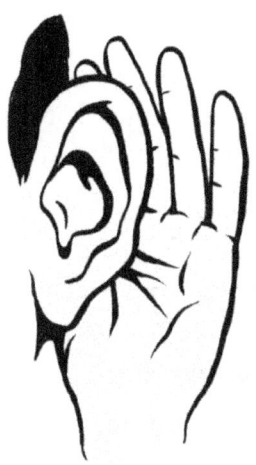

3) Listen

Listening is arguably the most important aspect to a successful career in customer service. Customers do not want to be interrupted or talked down to. They want to have their concerns heard by someone who genuinely cares about their happiness and is willing and able to help them.

Take the time to listen to the customer and validate what they are saying. Use confirming phrases periodically to let the customer know that you are paying attention and understand what they are trying to convey.

Here are some examples of confirming phrases/words:

- *"Okay"*

- *"I see."*

- *"I understand."*

- *"Alright"*

Allow the customer to tell their full story before you jump in. After the customer gets their side of the story out they will feel in a better position to let you speak.

4) Apologize

An upset customer needs an apology more than anything. Even though an apology doesn't necessarily change what happened, they still want to hear that you are sincerely sorry for what occurred.

It is appropriate to say something such as:

- *"I wish there is something I could have done to prevent that from happening."*

- *"I am so sorry this happened."*

- *"I'm sorry to hear that."*

- *"I apologize about the mistake."*

- *"I'm sorry about this."*

It is important to apologize even when nothing major happened. Every call deserves an apology, even if it was the customer who made a mistake. Do not blame the customer for making an error.

For example, if the customer ordered the wrong color item:

"I'm sorry that the blue yoga mat isn't working for you. Let's see what we can do to get you the black one instead."

It was not your fault that the customer ordered the wrong color, but apologizing could still be the difference between a satisfied customer and an unhappy one.

Here are some helpful phrases for apologizing for the customer's mistake:

- *"I'm sorry for any confusion."*

- *"I'm sorry the product isn't working out for you."*

- *"I'm sorry the product isn't filling your needs."*

5) Keep the Lines of Communication Open

If you have ever called customer service and been disconnected, you know how helpless it can feel when you don't know how to get back in touch with the same person. Customers want to know how they can get back to you if they have additional questions or if things don't go as planned. They need a life line and you can provide just that!

Find out what the customer's preferred method of communication is. Some people are unable to use certain methods, so be flexible. Make note of the preferred method so you remember how to get back in touch with them.

Within your company's guidelines and abilities, offer the customer:

- Your name

- Your direct phone number

- Your email address

- URL where they can chat with a representative

- Alternative contact information if you are going to be unavailable

Giving customers your contact information also elicits trust. It gives you some accountability in the eyes of the customer and shows them you are not trying to hide or avoid helping them.

6) Use Small Talk

There is bound to be downtime during a conversation with a customer. You may be waiting for a carrier to un-box something so the customer can get a better look. The customer may be waiting to get more information from someone on their end. Whatever the case may be, take the opportunity to chat with the customer. This will make the silence less awkward and provide a bonding opportunity.

Stay away from controversial topics such as politics or religion. Stick to things such as the weather, sports, or attractions in the caller's location.

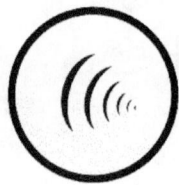

Ask the customer opened-ended questions such as:

- *"What is your weather like this time of year?"*

- *"How's your football team doing this season?"*

- *"Do you have any exciting plans for the weekend?"*

Look for things you might have in common with the customer:

- *"I see you live in Florida. I vacationed there last year and it was beautiful!"*

- *"You live in South Dakota? I hear you guys have gotten a lot of snow already this season."*

- *"I have this same item at home and I love it!"*

- *"I've been thinking of ordering this same item. What do you think of it?"*

Not all customers will respond well to small talk. Do not continue if the customer does not sound engaged. Some people are not comfortable chatting with strangers. If that is the impression you get, discontinue the discussion. You don't want the customer to be annoyed that their call took longer than necessary because you were busy chatting with them. Take a look at Tip #44 about Matching the Customer's Pace for help.

7) Be Empathetic

Empathy is the ability to recognize and share the feelings of others, and it is extremely important in a customer service environment. Customers want to have their feelings acknowledged and feel like you care about their thoughts.

One common hurdle customer service professionals often encounter when showing empathy is sounding too scripted. For tips on avoiding sounding scripted, check out Tip #27.

Some examples of how to show empathy are:

- *"I can see where you are coming from."*

- *"I would be upset too."*

- *"I'm sure that must have been upsetting."*

- *"I can see how upsetting this is."*

- *"You have every right to be upset."*

- *"I understand how disappointed you must be."*

- *"Let me see how we can make this right."*

Using words such as "let's" and "us" are helpful to show partnership with the customer. It shows the customer that you are in it together!

- *"Let's see how the factory can fix this problem for us."*

- *"Let's find out what can be done for us."*

All of these phrases help you build rapport with the customer. If the customer feels comfortable with you they will be more cooperative in finding a solution.

8) Ask Questions

Customers are giving you the information they feel is important. However, they might be leaving out important details. You are the expert; you know what information is needed to best help the customer. What details do you feel are important? By asking questions you are finding out the full story and allowing yourself to create the best solution possible.

For example, a customer calls with a request to return an item. Without asking questions this is how the conversation might go:

> CUSTOMER: "I want to return my order."
>
> CUSTOMER SERVICE: "Ok. I will request authorization from the returns department. You will be responsible for $9.99 in shipping charges to return it. Please keep all of the packaging."

Based on this conversation, why did the customer want to make a return? Was the product damaged? Did the customer receive the wrong item? Is the item mis-advertised on your company's website? It is impossible to know based on the above conversation.

Now look at the conversation when you ask questions to find out more details about why they want to return the item.

> CUSTOMER SERVICE: "I'm sorry to hear the product isn't working out for you. What is the reason you want to return it?"
>
> CUSTOMER: "It's the wrong color."
>
> CUSTOMER SERVICE: "I understand. I just want to find out more information so we can get this straightened out for you. Did we ship you the wrong color or did you mean to order a different one?"
>
> CUSTOMER: "It's the color I ordered, but I was expecting a darker shade of blue."

By asking questions you are able to get a lot of valuable information. If the shade of blue on your company's website is misrepresented you can request to have it changed. If the wrong color was sent out you can alert the factory or warehouse to the mistake. Perhaps you are just dealing with an overly particular customer, but it is also possible that there is a deeper issue that you can help address.

The extra information you get from the customer by asking questions can help prevent similar problems from happening again in the future.

The types of questions you ask depends a lot on the situation, but here are some ideas:

- *"What happened next?"*

- *"Can you describe….?"*

- *"What happens if you….?"*

- *"Can you explain to me…?"*

- *"How long has this been occurring?"*

- *"Please tell me about the….”*

Asking questions also shows the customer that you are interested in their problem. It can help you get to the root of the problem and develop creative solutions.

9) Avoid Saying No

Customers do not like to hear the word no. Even if what follows it is positive, customers will have an immediate negative reaction to hearing the word no. The commonly used phrase "no problem" can elicit a negative response, because the first thing the person hears is "no."

Rather than saying "no" to what the customer is asking for, try to soften it a little using the following phrases:

- *"What I **can** do is…."*

- *"I would certainly do that for you if I could, but…"*

- *"I understand, but unfortunately that isn't an option."*

- *"I don't think that will be possible, but…"*

- *"What we **are** able to do is…."*

The word "no" really sticks out for people. It can make an already-upset customer even more upset. This tip goes hand in hand with Tip #10 (offer alternative solutions). Use them together to calm down upset customers, and make sure the conversation stays productive!

10) Offer Alternative Solutions

Even if you cannot give the customer exactly what they want, make sure you are offering them alternative options. Focus on what you **can** do for them instead of what you cannot do.

If the customer says: "I want a replacement here tomorrow" a typical response may be "No, I can't do that." Instead, say something like "I would certainly do that for you if I could, but unfortunately that is not an option. What I can do for you is ask the warehouse to ship your order out within 48 hours. I will also request priority shipping once it does go out. I'd be happy to email you the tracking number once it ships out. Does that sound fair to you?"

Obviously you need to work within your company's policies. Perhaps you have different options that you can use at your discretion, or maybe you need to get manager approval.

Here are some ideas of alternative solutions:

- Discount to keep as-is

- Exchange the product

- Complimentary product/service

- Discount for delays/problems

- Expedited shipping on replacement

- Extra packaging or inspection on replacement

- Step-by-step updates on the replacement order

Offering alternative solutions shows the customer you are willing to help them and can keep them from shutting down. Customers often get frustrated when they are only offered one "approved solution" that may or may not work for them. Offering alternatives is a good way to keep the customer on your side!

11) Ask the Customer What They Think is Fair

When you reach a stalemate in the conversation, asking the customer what they feel would be fair can be a good way to keep the conversation moving. Not all solutions are created equal. What works for one customer might not work for another. The only way to know is to ask the customer what they want.

By asking the customer for input, you are making them a part of the solution. They are more likely to feel happy about the outcome if they had a hand in making the decision.

Use these phrases to put the ball in the customer's court:

- *"What do you feel would be a fair resolution?"*

- *"What do you think is a reasonable outcome?"*

- *"What kind of solution are you looking for?"*

- *"What do you think is fair?"*

- *"What kind of resolution do you think is fair?"*

- *"What kind of fair agreement can we come to?"*

Often times, what the customer comes back with will be less than what you were prepared to give them. This question lets the customer set the bar. The customer will also feel in power because they are being asked how they feel and what they want, rather than having a solution forced upon them.

If the customer replies with something that you cannot provide, go back through the negotiation process. Be sure to avoid saying no (see Tip #9) and offer alternative solutions (see Tip #10). Eventually you will come to a mutually agreeable solution.

12) Don't overpromise

Not overpromising is an important rule to follow when dealing with any customer. Be realistic when offering solutions. Do not just agree to what the customer wants without being able to follow through on it. Quickly agreeing with the customer to get them off of the phone will only result in another call to your office. The customer will likely be even more upset because they have been let down again.

Only tell the customer something if you are POSITIVE it can actually happen. Wait until you have verified that something happened before you confirm it with the customer.

For example, if your warehouse said an order would ship out in the morning, call them and verify that it did before telling the customer that their order shipped. Just because someone says that something will happen does not mean that it actually will.

Some customers may try to get you to make promises to them. Here are some phrases to use if you are in this situation:

- *"I don't want to make promises that I am not 100% sure I can keep."*

- *"I will make every effort to make this happen, but I cannot guarantee it."*

- *"I will do everything in my power to meet your request, but I don't want to make a promise."*

Overpromising something that you cannot deliver on only sets the customer up for another disappointment!

13) Offer Preventative Measures

Customers want to hear what is going to be done to make sure their problem doesn't happen again. Often times, telling a customer that you are going to report the problem to quality control will make them feel like some good is coming from their experience.

If the customer's complaint is that something arrived damaged, offer to have the factory use extra packaging on the replacement order. If their complaint is that their order arrived in the wrong color, offer to have the replacement order inspected prior to shipping.

Whatever preventative measures you offer, be sure that you aren't promising something that you can't deliver on. Be realistic in what you offer the customer. (See Tip #12 Don't Overpromise)

14) Give a Final Offer to Help

During the closing of the call, it is important to ask the customer if they need further assistance with anything. By asking them if they have any further questions, it will prompt them to ask any remaining questions while they are on the phone. This not only provides a confident feeling to the customer, but it also prevents them from calling back to your office again. This means less hassle for the customer and fewer calls that need to be answered on your end.

Here are some potential ways to give a final offer of help:

- *"Have I answered all of your questions today?"*

- *"Have all of your questions been answered?"*

- *"Has everything been handled to your satisfaction?"*

These phrases not only fill the requirement of giving a final offer of help, but they also prompt an answer of yes. This is better than asking *"Is there anything else I can do for you?"* because that question prompts an answer of no. (Also see Tip #9 Avoid Saying No).

15) Thank the Customer for Their Business

No matter what your company does, it relies on customers in order to stay in business. Customers are truly the life-line of every business.

Regardless of the nature of the call, you should thank the customer for doing business with your company.

Right after a customer presents their problem to you, say something like: *"I am sorry for the problem. We certainly appreciate your business and I'm sorry this problem happened."*

You can also interject the "thank you for your business" during the closing of a call. At the end of the call, thank the caller again for calling (see Tip #2) and thank them for their business. This is the last impression they will have of your organization, and it is important to end the call on a good note.

An easy way to do this is to say: "Thank you so much for calling. We here at XYZ Company truly appreciate your business!" or "Thank you for taking the time to talk to me today. We really appreciate your business."

16)   Recap the Conversation

Once a resolution has been reached it is important to recap the plan of action with the customer. Going over the resolution that was reached and recapping the next step will clear up any miscommunications. It is a good way to make sure that you and the customer are on the same page.

Here are some helpful phrases to use in order to recap the conversation:

- *"Just so we are on the same page, this is what we are going to do…"*

- *"To recap, first we are going to…."*

- *"To go over our plan, the first step in fixing this problem is to…."*

- *"As we discussed, the next thing we are going to do is…."*

- *"To sum up what we talked about…."*

- *"Just to summarize…."*

- *"As we talked about, the next step is…"*

If the customer disagrees with something mentioned during the recap you may have to go back and refine the solution. While repeating the action plan might feel redundant, it is an important step in the customer service process. If you skip this step the customer may call back when things do not go as they expected them to.

17) Build Trust

Keeping the lines of communication open (Tip #5) is a great first step towards building trust with a customer. It shows the customer that you are available, ready, and willing to help them resolve their problem.

Another great step in building trust is to follow through with what you've told the customer you are going to do. Each time you follow through on a promise it helps the customer trust you even more.

If you told the customer you would call them by the end of the day, be sure to call them even if you don't have an update. A simple "I am still working on your issue, but I wanted to make sure to touch base with you as promised" will go a long way.

When you are offering options keep in mind that your goal is to build trust. A sure way to erode trust is to make promises you cannot keep (see Tip #12). If you can't come through for the customer they will have a harder time believing the next thing you tell them. This can make future dealings with the customer much more difficult.

Having a trusting relationship with customers can make interactions with them much easier. Customers will have a much harder time being rude or angry towards you if they have already formed a relationship with you. Work on building their trust so that if there comes a time when you need their cooperation they will be more likely to give it to you.

18) Be Proactive

Chances are you answer a lot of customer service calls. This makes you an expert in your field and it is time to put that knowledge to use! You can probably predict the next question that is about to come out of your customer's mouth. Use that to your advantage by being proactive and answering the question before it is asked.

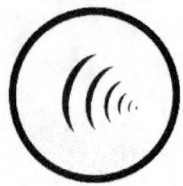

For example, after you tell the customer you are going to enter a replacement order they often ask when it will ship out. Instead of saying "I entered a replacement order for you" and then stopping, try "I entered a replacement order and it should ship within 1-2 days." By doing this you have reduced the number of questions the customer needs to ask.

Being proactive does not end when the customer hangs up the phone. What did you tell the customer was going to happen next? Be proactive to make sure those things actually happen. The only thing worse than disappointing a customer is disappointing them twice. (See Tip #12 about not overpromising.)

If you told the customer:

> "Your replacement will ship within 1-2 days" then set your calendar or write yourself a note to check back on the status of the replacement. (For more tips on following up, see Tip #20)

> "The delivery person will reattempt delivery between 1 and 4 pm tomorrow" then set your calendar or write yourself a note to call the carrier at 12:30 pm to make sure the driver is still coming as scheduled.

> "The item will be back in stock in 2-3 weeks" then set your calendar or write yourself a note to check back in 1 ½ weeks to see if the item is still expected back in stock.

Being proactive is a great way to set your customer service apart from the rest. This is how you can amaze your customers!

You might feel like this creates more work. In some ways, perhaps it does. However, if your goal is excellent customer service then it is worth it! If you follow up on something and find out that your plan is not going as expected, you have time to try to fix it before the customer gets involved. Finding out about a problem before the customer does puts the control in your hands. If the problem cannot be fixed before the customer finds out about it, at least you have time to come up with a new plan of how to deal with the customer.

The other option is waiting until the customer calls you because things didn't go as expected. In that situation, you might be caught off-guard and not know how to deal with the issue on the spot. Worst of all, the customer is even more upset because they already had problems and are now being troubled again.

While it is true that the customer might get a different customer service representative when they call the second time, that doesn't mean the problem will go away. The customer's problem is your company's problem, regardless of who the customer speaks with.

19) Show Customers, Don't Tell

Customers don't want to feel like you are giving them orders. This can happen a lot, especially when you are trying to tell them how to fix something or put something together. You've probably had the same conversation a hundred times, so it's second nature to you. This can cause you to skip important details or oversimplify the process.

If possible, get a copy of the same instructions the customer has. Walk them through it from the view point of a customer who is doing it for the first time.

Rather than giving short orders such as: *"Plug the cord into the AV port in the back"* try being more descriptive: *"Do you see the port on the back of the unit? It should be second from the left. Take the cord with the yellow end and plug it in there."*

In the first situation you gave the customer an order they might not understand. In the second scenario you showed exactly them what to do.

20) Follow Up

Keep a written or electronic note of what further steps need to be taken for each customer. Some companies have software that helps you do this. Other situations might call for keeping track of this manually.

Here are some ideas for keeping track manually.

Use file folders:

- Designate three folders for the current day

    - One folder for first thing in the morning

    - One folder for just before or after lunch

    - One folder for before you leave for the day

- Designate additional folders: one for each day of the week and one for the following week.

When you handle a customer service call that requires further follow up, write the details on a piece of paper and put the paper in the folder that corresponds with the time you need to follow up on it next.

> For example, a customer calls to report a late delivery. You find out that the delivery should be there by the end of the day. Put this order in your "end of day" folder. When you look in this folder towards the end of the day you will see this order and know to follow up. Look at the folder with enough time to call the customer, and allow time to contact the carrier if they still haven't arrived.

> In another situation you find out an order is late. You notify the customer that their order should ship in one week. Put this order in your "next week" folder. When you open the folder next week you will know that you need to check on the order again.

Each morning when you arrive look at all of the orders in your "morning" file and in your folder for that day of the week.

If you do not want to use physical folders you can setup a similar system using different folders on your computer.

To use folders on your computer:

- Put the order number in a document and into the appropriate folder

- Move and delete orders as needed

You can also use calendar reminders within your email program. This works great if you need an audible reminder.

To use calendar reminders:

- Set appointments in your calendar to remind you which orders to look at

- Be sure appointments are set as "free" otherwise someone who tries to schedule an actual meeting with you will find your calendar full

- Set a reminder so you are alerted to each appointment

Whichever method you choose, the point is the same: check in on your orders frequently so you can ensure that things are progressing as expected. This helps you be proactive (Tip #18) and build trust with the customer (Tip #17).

21) Mirror What the Customer is Saying

Customers want to be heard, and they want to make sure you truly understand what they are saying. A great way to achieve this is to mirror what the customer tells you. When the customer gives you information, repeat it back to them to make sure you understand correctly.

For example, an angry customer is telling you about a problem with the ceiling fan they ordered. "There is a four inch crack in one of the blades and I'm missing two of the screws labeled 'A' and one of screw 'B'."

A good way to mirror this is to say: "Just to make sure I understand, there is a crack in one of the blades and you are missing two of screw 'A' and one of screw 'B'."

This offers the customer an opportunity to correct you if you misunderstood and also shows them you were listening.

Here are some helpful phrases to use when you mirror the customer:

- *"What I think you are saying is…."*

- *"Just to be sure I understand…."*

- *"Just to make sure I have this right…."*

- *"So what you are saying is…."*

- *"Can I confirm what you said so I'm sure I got it right?"*

- *"As I understand…"*

If you misunderstood or wrote down the wrong information the customer has an opportunity to correct you.

22) Keep the Customer Up-to-Date

When you look through your folders and find orders that need to be followed up on, don't forget to give the customer an update. You've already done the work, now tell the customer what is going on!

In many instances, calling the customer won't change the outcome. Ideally, when you follow up on orders you will find that things are going exactly as expected. The difference is that when you confirm this with the customer you are giving them added reassurance and faith in your company.

Many of these conversations are just "FYI's" (for your information).

Here are some ways to have this conversation with the customer:

- *"I just wanted to confirm everything is on track."*

- *"Just to let you know, things are going as expected."*

- *"I'm calling with an update on your order."*

23) Use the Customer's Name

Using the customer's name in conversation is a great way to connect with them. Hearing their name can make people calm down when they are in a tense situation.

If you have a hard time remembering the name of the person you are speaking to, write it down at the beginning of the conversation. Not only does this help ensure you use the correct name, but it also provides a visual reminder of how many customers you help each day.

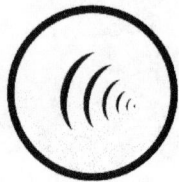

If you need to ask the customer's name again, here are some ways to say it:

- *"I'm sorry. Could I get your name again?"*

- *"Can you repeat your name for me again?"*

- *"I'm so forgetful—would you mind telling me your name again?"*

- *"I'm sorry. I didn't catch your name."*

- *"If you don't mind, can you tell me your name again?"*

The closing of a call is a great time to use the customer's name:

- *"Thank you for calling, Alex. Have a great day!"*

- *"Thank you for calling us today, Anna. Please let me know if there is anything else I can do for you."*

- *"We appreciate your call, Megan. I look forward to working with you in the future!"*

Using the customer's name too often during a conversation can sound awkward and rehearsed. Aim to use the customer's name between one and three times during each conversation. This is frequent enough to show the customer you were paying attention but not so much that it gets uncomfortable.

24) Take Ownership

Customers are used to hearing excuses:

"The technician got hung up with a customer, so he can't make it to your house."

"The manufacturer just told me a machine broke down, so your order won't be finished in time."

"The truck broke down, so your delivery is going to be late."

What all of these have in common is that they pass the blame onto another party. That might make you feel better, but it doesn't really offer the customer any solace. Chances are the customer doesn't care whose mistake it was. As far as they are concerned it doesn't really matter who messed up.

Here are some phrases to use to take responsibility for the problem without passing blame:

- *"I am sorry for our error."*

- *"We made a mistake."*

- *"I'm sorry we missed the mark."*

- *"I'm sorry we fell short of your expectations."*

- *"It was our responsibility and we didn't come through."*

25) Look for Patterns

You are the company's first line of defense against problems. If you notice the same problem happening again and again, speak up. You have the information your company needs in order to improve. Perhaps there are mistakes on the company website that need to be corrected. Maybe there is a quality issue with a particular supplier that needs to be addressed. These are all things that won't be addressed if you don't speak up.

Some companies have computer systems that allow each representative to track the issues they handle. If yours doesn't, keep track of issues manually. If you begin to notice a recurring issue with a product, supplier, service, or shipping company, keep track of the order or account numbers. It is important to have details so if your manager asks for your opinion about a topic, you have something to back up your feelings. Then you can say, "I've had 10 complaints about this product in the last month" rather than, "A lot of people complain about that item."

Here are some examples of patterns to watch for:

- Frequent problems on a certain item

- Recurring complaints about a particular freight company

- Requests for clarification about a product or feature

- Incorrect details on the company website

- Recurring complaints about a specific problem

In many instances, issues can be corrected with clarifying information on the company's website. Having up-to-date and accurate information on the website can prevent a lot of calls to customer service and lessen the customer's frustration!

Looking for patterns is a great tool for you to set yourself apart from other customer service professionals and add value to your team!

26) Have an Upbeat Tone

The tone of your voice gives the customer their first impression of you. If you sound bored, upset, or annoyed, the customer is going to sense that. Sometimes this can be easier said than done (especially if you answer a lot of phone calls), but there are some things you can do.

Here are some tips on how to perk up your tone:

- Take a deep breath before answering a call.

- Stand up and stretch between phone calls.

- Listen to upbeat music (make sure the volume isn't too loud though).

- Put a smile on your face. (see Tip #52)

- Greet each customer as if you were meeting them in person.

Answering each call with an upbeat tone can help you start out each call on the right note.

27) Avoid Sounding Scripted

No one likes to deal with a customer service representative that sounds like a robot. Put some enthusiasm in your voice, and have a genuine conversation with the customer. If you use the same phrases repeatedly they can start to sound a bit stale. Try mixing things up by slightly modifying the phrases you use.

Depending on the line of business your company is in there might be various things that you are required to say. Rather than immediately jumping into a rehearsed script, let the customer know that you need to go over the required details.

Here are some helpful phrases:

- *"There are a few things I need to cover before we get started."*

- *"Before I help you, I need to let you know that…."*

- *"Real quick, I need to tell you that…."*

- *"Before we get started, there are a couple things I'm required to tell you."*

- *"I am required to cover a few things before we move on."*

- *"Let me get these formalities out of the way."*

These phrases let the customer know that you need to make certain statements before helping them. It gives them an indication that you will not sound like a robot for the entire call!

28) Pay Attention

Sometimes customers won't come out and tell you what they want. They might not think it is an option or are too embarrassed or upset to ask. Pay attention to how they are acting and what they are saying (even if they are saying it to someone else.)

Often times the person who is calling you is not the decision maker. They might be calling on behalf of their boss, spouse, or parent. When you tell them something they relay it to the other party. You can often tell a lot by overhearing that conversation and use what you learn to offer appealing solutions.

When you pay attention to what the customer is saying they might give you an idea of what they truly want as a resolution.

Here are some tips on how to pay attention to your customers:

- Put all other work aside so it doesn't distract you.

- Listen to what the customer is saying (Tip #3) and to any background conversations they are having.

- Take notes so you don't forget any important details.

- Recap the conversation (Tip #16) to confirm you understand.

Paying attention to the customer is a great way to build trust (Tip #17) which can help them be more cooperative with you.

29) Have a Positive Attitude

A positive attitude is a great asset to have in your work and personal life. Not only can it make you happier, but it will likely have the same effect on those around you. When you work in customer service you need to take extra steps to ensure you maintain a positive attitude.

It can be difficult to maintain a positive attitude, but here are some tips to help:

- Post pictures of your friends and family: Unless you're independently wealthy and work for the fun of it, you work to make money to support yourself and your family. You work because it allows you to spend time with your friends and family, doing things you enjoy. Put pictures of your family and friends up in your work area to remind you of all the good things you have in life. This can help you keep a positive attitude when you are having a rough day or dealing with a difficult customer.

- Display motivational quotes in your work area: Many people have shared profound thoughts about life and work. Find your favorite motivational quotes and post them. Look for a motivational quote day-by-day calendar so you get fresh inspiration each day. Find motivational posters to hang on the wall. Make positivity the focal point of your office!

- Make a daily positive declaration: Start each day by writing down or verbalizing three positive things that happened the previous day. By focusing on the things you are thankful for you can start to train your brain to see the positives.

- Keep positive feedback: Sometimes it can feel like all you ever hear are negative comments. Deep down you know that isn't true, but sometimes it is hard to remember that. When you do get positive feedback from coworkers, your boss, or customers, keep it close by. When you are having a particularly difficult time read these comments and remember all of the good things you've done.

- Focus on the positives: It can be easy to get stuck in "complaint mode." Everything that happens and everything that someone says spurs a negative thought in your mind. Before speaking, think about how you can turn your actions into a positive. When someone says something negative, immediately say something positive. When "Negative-Nancy" in your office says, "Ugh, that customer was horrible! She wouldn't stop talking for 20 minutes!" reply with, "Looks like you're 20 minutes closer to break time!" Negative-Nancy was waiting for you to ask questions about her difficult customer, but instead you turned the conversation positive and showed Nancy you weren't interested in reliving her tough call. Do this enough and Nancy will either start complaining to someone else or stop complaining at all.

- Stay away from negative people: Negativity can be toxic. If you spend all your time with people who are complaining you will naturally start complaining too. If you've tried focusing on the positives to shift your coworkers' attitudes and it isn't working, you might need to avoid associating with them so much.

- Make a declaration: Sometimes people don't realize how negative they are. If you're too embarrassed to point it out, make a declaration of your own and hope that they will follow suit. "I am making an effort to be more positive."

30) Calm Customers Down

There is no avoiding escalated situations completely; you're going to work with angry customers from time-to-time. When customers are yelling it is very difficult to solve their problems. It's usually best to let them get it all out first before trying to talk to them. However, some customers may not let you get a word in. If they've gone over the whole story and are still yelling, these phrases can come in handy:

- *"I want to help you, but I can't do that until you stop yelling."*

- *"I understand you are upset, but I need you to calm down so I can help you."*

- *"Let's have a peaceful discussion so we can figure this out together."*

- *"I am here to help you, but I can't do that unless you work with me."*

- *"Please give me the chance to help you."*

These phrases help you acknowledge the customer's feelings and appeal for them to calm down.

31) Learn How to Handle Escalated Situations

If you do this job long enough is inevitable that you will deal with some tense situations. Many customers will immediately ask for your supervisor, before even giving you a chance to help them. Rather than trying to pass these customers off to someone else, try to get them to work with you. If you transfer them to your supervisor from the beginning and your supervisor isn't able to help them, there is little room to go from there. Let the customer start with you so there is room to escalate the call if needed.

Use these helpful phrases to try to get upset customers to work with you rather than your supervisor.

- *"My supervisor isn't available at the moment, but I am and I would love to help you."*

- *"I am authorized to speak on behalf of my manager, so please let me try to help you first."*

- *"I can offer you the same solutions that my manager can."*

- *"My supervisor is in a meeting, but if you allow me to, I can help fix your problem."*

- *"My manager would have to get back to you, but I am available to help you now."*

Your manager will be thankful that you try to help customers before passing them on to him or her. This is another way you can add value to your team. Be recognized as someone who can handle tough customers and doesn't shy away from difficult situations.

32) Start Fresh

If you are not careful it can be easy to let one bad call ruin your entire day. Each new call deserves your full attention. It is unfair to let your last bad call have a negative impact on the interaction with your next customer. Make a conscious effort to "start fresh" before every call.

Here are some things you can do to help yourself start each call with renewed energy:

- Stand up and stretch

- Take a deep breath to clear your mind

- Count to 10 before moving on to the next task

- Take a drink of water

Find out what works for you--just do something to clear your mind so that when you pick up the phone you are starting with a clean slate!

33) Set Expectations

Many repeat phone calls happen because the customer is not clear about what is going to happen next. Or if they do know what is going to happen next, they don't understand exactly when it is going to happen.

Rather than telling a customer: "I will call you back when I have more news" tell them **when** they can expect your phone call. If you aren't sure, give them a time frame when they will hear from you, even if you don't have an answer. A good alternative is to say: "I will call you back when I have more news. It might take a few hours, but you'll hear from me by the end of the day, either way." As always, avoid overpromising things to customers. (See Tip #12)

Here are some good phrases to use when setting expectations:

- *"You can expect to hear back from me in 2-3 hours."*

- *"I will let you know by the end of the day."*

- *"You'll hear from me again on Wednesday."*

- *"Expect an email from me within the hour."*

- *"Even if I don't have an answer for you, I'll touch base with you by the end of the day."*

- *"I'll get back to you no later than tomorrow at 10:00 am."*

Setting expectations is an easy thing you can do to improve your customer service. If you were the customer, you would appreciate someone telling you what to expect! This can clear up a lot of confusion and prevent the customer from calling back later when they are confused or unclear about what is going to happen next.

34) Don't "Blind" Transfer

There are often times when you need to transfer a customer to someone else. When you make a transfer it is important that the customer *and* the person you are transferring them to know why.

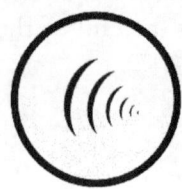

Sometimes this happens when you have the customer on the line. If that is the case, simply tell them who you need to transfer them to and why.

- *"I need to transfer you to our returns department so they can process a return authorization for you."*

Other times it happens when the customer is on hold. If the customer is on hold, get them back on the line before you transfer them.

- *"Thank you for holding. I need to transfer you to our escalations department so they can look at your order."*

When the person you are transferring them to picks up, give them the back story. Then when you connect the two parties they will both have an understanding of what needs to be done.

- *"I have the customer, Katie, on hold. I am going to transfer her to you. Her order number is 5100796 and she needs to process a return."*

This makes for a much more natural conversation and prevents the customer from having to repeat their entire story to the person you transfer them to.

35) Ask Permission Before Hold

As a customer there's nothing worse than being on the phone and suddenly hearing elevator music. If you have to put a customer on hold ask them prior to doing so. Always tell them why you are putting them on hold and approximately how long it will take.

- *"Do you mind if I put you on hold? I need to call the carrier; it should take 1-2 minutes."*

- *"If I could put you on hold for 2-3 minutes I will call manufacturing and find out what is happening."*

- *"Is it okay if I put you on hold for about 2 minutes? I need to get some help from one of my coworkers."*

At this point the customer might tell you they prefer not to hold. Maybe they are in the middle of something else and it is inconvenient for them to wait. In that case, find out how you can best get back to them.

- *"What's the best way for me to get in touch with you when I'm off the phone?"*

- *"I can let you know when I'm off the phone. What's the best way to get back to you?"*

If the hold is taking longer than expected, go back to the customer to see if they still want to wait.

- *"I'm sorry, this is taking longer than expected. Do you want to continue to wait?"*

- *"I apologize for the long delay. Is it more convenient for me to call you back?"*

- *"I'm sorry, I am still waiting for information. Do you want to continue to wait?"*

36) Thank the Customer for Holding

When you put a customer on hold (for any reason), be sure to apologize or thank them for holding when you come back on the line. The customer has been inconvenienced in some way and it is up to you to make them less upset about it. The following phrases can help you transition from having a customer on hold to going back to helping them.

Use these phrases when you take a customer off hold:

- *"Thank you so much for holding."*

- *"I apologize for the long hold."*

- *"Thank you for your patience during that hold."*

- *"I'm sorry for the delay."*

- *"Thanks for your understanding during that long hold."*

- *"I'm very sorry I had to put you on hold."*

- *"Thank you for holding while I got that information for you."*

These phrases show the customer that you value their time. This can go a long way towards establishing rapport with a customer. As you know, establishing rapport is a good way to get a customer to work with you on finding a resolution to their problem. Get them to work with you instead of working against you!

37) Be Professional

Sometimes it can be difficult to keep your composure. When customers are yelling at you it is tempting to yell back. However, losing your cool won't help in that type of situation. The best thing you can do is stay professional.

Here are some valuable tips for maintaining professionalism:

- Count to Ten: When you're in a tense situation, take a few seconds to calm down. Try counting to ten. It can prevent you from saying something you'll regret.

- Breathe Deep: Breathing techniques can help you calm down when you are in "fight or flight" mode.

- Put the Customer on Hold: When things are beginning to escalate too far, sometimes the best thing you can do is put the customer on hold. Be sure to ask the customer if this is okay first (see Tip #35).

- Bite Your Tongue: If you question whether you should say something, it is probably best not to say it. Resist the urge to fight back.

It is important to be professional in your email and voicemail correspondence as well. You can find tips on using voicemail appropriately in Tip #45 and following email etiquette in Tip #46.

38) Be Organized

Customers don't want to hear you fumble to find the information you need. If there is information you need on a regular basis make sure you know where you can find it. Keep important numbers, forms, and instructions nearby so you can find them at a moment's notice.

Here are some ways to become more organized:

- Create multiple folders, based on topic.

- Post frequently used documents to your cubicle or office wall.

- If you change workspaces often, put your information in a binder so you can take it with you.

- Keep all of your needed materials in one spot so you can easily find them.

- File papers promptly so you always know the right place to look for them.

If you have an influx of paperwork that needs to be addressed, get multiple trays or folders. One way to organize them is by using three folders: READ, DO, FILE.

Items in your "do" file require more attention and time. Items in your "read" file require focused time and quiet. However, the items in your "file" file can often be addressed with little energy. If you are on hold, you can take a few seconds to file the things that are in this folder.

When you have quiet time you can absorb the information you are reading from the "read" file. If you need to take further action on it but don't have time for it immediately, put it in the "do" file. If you don't need to do anything with it at that moment, but it needs to be filed for further reference, put it in your "file" folder.

The real time savings comes from not looking at the same material multiple times. If you have a few minutes of quiet you can quickly find something to work on. If you are looking for something to do with minimal attention you can find it quickly. This is better than spending all of your time looking through your paperwork.

39) Avoid Awkward Silence

When you have a customer on the phone there are inevitably times when there won't be anything to talk about. Perhaps you are inputting notes into the system, looking for documentation, or filling out paperwork. Sitting in silence can be painful for both you and the customer.

Here are a couple alternatives to fill the quiet times:

- Use Small Talk: Chat with the customer about various topics; they don't have to be problem-related. (See Tip #6).

- Put the Customer on Hold: Sometimes you won't be able to maintain the conversation and still get the things done you need to do. If you need to focus on something else, you might be better off putting the customer on hold. Just be sure to ask the customer first! (See Tip #35).

If you need to be quiet and don't want to put the customer on hold, tell the customer so they aren't concerned that they have been disconnected.

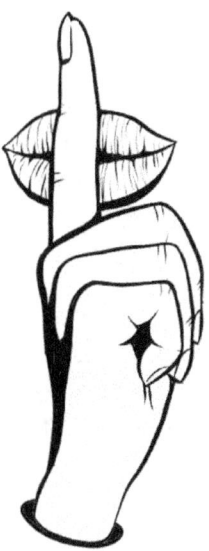

- *"I'm going to be silent for a minute, but don't worry, we didn't get disconnected."*

- *"I'm not going to talk for a minute, but I'm here if you need me."*

- *"Is it okay if I'm silent for a couple minutes?"*

- *"I'm going to be quiet for a couple minutes, but let me know if you need anything."*

40) Learn Everything You Can

By learning everything you can about your company's product or service, you are making yourself more valuable to your customer. The more you know the less likely you are to give the customer misinformation. It also means you will not need to put the customer on hold to ask someone else.

If you learn unusual tidbits, be sure to write them down so you have it for next time you encounter that situation. If your company has a training manual, take notes so you remember what you have learned. If your company has a catalog, write down product-specific information in the margins. These references will become a great resource for you as you continue your work.

Your coworkers can be a great resource as you attempt to learn everything you can about your job. Ask those sitting nearby for advice, or consider getting a mentor. To find out more about mentors, check out Tip #47 (Find a Mentor).

41) Ditch Negativity

Is there a person in your office who is constantly complaining? Who manages to find something bad in every situation? Who moans and groans after each and every phone call? Who rehashes every angry conversation they have?

While it might feel good to "get things off your chest," at some point it is doing more harm than good. Negativity is toxic and spreads from one person to the next. Do your best to avoid people like this. If you are sitting next to one, consider asking for a transfer to a different spot. If you cannot move away from them, maybe you need to point out their negativity. Sometimes people don't realize how negative they are. If you're too embarrassed to point it out, make a declaration of your own and hope that they will follow suit. "I am making an effort to be more positive."

Is it you who is spreading negativity around your office? You do not want to be known as the person who brings everyone else down. If you need some help turning your attitude around, go over Tip #29 (Have a Positive Attitude) again.

42) Let Customers Vent

Dealing with angry customers can be difficult at times. Sometimes all upset customers want is to know that they are being heard. If you try to cut them off right away it will only upset them more. When they get upset, don't interrupt them. Letting them vent can ease their stress and get the bad feelings out of the way. Once they are done telling their side of the story they will be better able to focus on how to work with you to resolve the problem.

Sometimes letting customers vent can involve being silent. They might not let you get a word in. In that case, just listen and try not to get too upset.

Other customers might be looking to engage you in an argument. Stay calm and avoid verbal arguments. When both parties are upset, little progress is usually made.

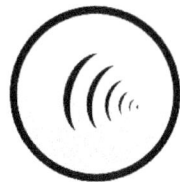

If the customer is prompting you for a response you can use these phrases:

- *"I am just trying to get the full story before we proceed."*

- *"As soon as you are done explaining what happened we can get this figured out."*

When they are finally done venting you need to calm them down so they can civilly work with you to find a resolution.

Here are some helpful phrases to use with customers who are done venting:

- *"Ok. Now that I have all the details, let's get this figured out."*

- *"Now that I know the full story, I'd like to help you."*

43) Be Sincere

Some people naturally sound sincere, while others may need to work at it a little bit. With a few small changes you can improve your sincerity and connect with your customers.

Using the customer's name in conversation is a very simple way to sound sincere. If you have trouble remembering each name, make a habit of writing it down at the beginning of each call. For more tips, read over Tip #23 again (Use the Customer's Name).

Be sure to give 100% of your attention to the customer. Put down any other work you are handling and invest yourself in talking to the customer. Customers can tell if you are occupied with something else and not paying attention to them! You can find more advice on this in Tip #28 (Pay Attention).

Asking questions is an important part of being sincere. By asking questions you are showing the customer that you care about the problem they are having. It also shows that you are paying attention and want to get more information in order to help them. You can learn more about asking questions in Tip #8 (Ask Questions).

44) Match the Customer's Pace

Many of the tips you've read so far add additional time to your interaction with the customer. What if they are clearly in a rush and are impatient? If you sense that the customer is in a hurry, do your best to handle the call swiftly.

Some customers get annoyed with chit-chat, while others think it provides a more personal experience. It is your job to figure out their preferred style and act accordingly. If you sense that your customer is in a hurry see what tasks can be done after they are off the phone. For example, normally you recap the next steps before hanging up (see Tip #16). If the customer is in a big hurry you can recap via email instead. Tell the customer to expect an email from you that will go over the next steps.

- *"I can tell that you are in a hurry, so I will email you with more information."*

- *"We've rushed through this call, so I will send you an email to make sure we didn't miss anything."*

On the other hand, you might get customers who want to talk and talk, long after you have handled their issues. If this happens you might need to use some of these phrases to get them off the phone.

- *"It's been great talking to you, but now I need to help the next person."*

- *"Sorry I can't chat longer. I have other customers to take care of."*

- *"If we've handled all of your issues, I need to hang up to help the next customer."*

- *"I'm being called away from my desk, so I need to get going."*

45) Use Voicemail Appropriately

Voicemail can be a very valuable tool but only when used correctly. When used appropriately it can help you communicate with customers, suppliers, and coworkers in an effective way.

Here are some things to keep in mind when using voicemail:

- Don't use voicemail to avoid confrontation. It can be tempting to use voicemail to tell customers bad news. It is easier than dealing with them over the phone because you don't have to listen to their immediate backlash. However, giving bad information in voicemail can make the customer angrier. It forces them to make another effort to contact you, and it gives them more time to fester about whatever bad news they received. You need to be available when you give bad news so you can calm them down and help do damage control.

- Make sure the customer is okay with voicemail. You should always ask the customer their preferred method of communication. Some people don't regularly check their voicemail. It really depends on the person, but it is up to you to find out in advance and use the preferred method. Ask the customer: "What is the best way to get back to you?" If they prefer a phone call, ask them if it is okay to leave the information in a message. "If I get your voicemail, is it okay if I leave you the tracking number in a message?"

- Prepare before leaving a voicemail. If you have important information to give in a voicemail, make sure you have it prepared before you call. Have all of the information handy so you can smoothly and clearly give the customer the details.

46) Follow Email Etiquette Rules

Email is an incredibly convenient tool for customer service professionals. That being said, there are certain rules you should always follow when using email to communicate with customers, coworkers, and external vendors/carriers:

- Never deliver bad news via email. If you do this, you do not have the opportunity to turn the problem into a positive interaction. The customer cannot tell your tone, hear the sincerity in your voice when you apologize, or air their concerns. Call the customer and use your excellent customer service skills to smooth over the situation. It might not be as bad as you imagine it to be.

- Keep emails short. If it takes more than a couple paragraphs to fully explain something, chances are it is too complex for an email. A long email will likely cause the customer to reply back with an equally long email. Before you know it, it becomes a vicious cycle.

- Be professional. Email does not convey tone and what you may think is funny may be interpreted as rude. Stay away from jokes, sarcasm, puns, and abbreviations. Do not be overly casual in emails either. This is not a time for you to say: "Hey Mel, it was like pulling teeth but I finally got an answer for ya." "Dear Melissa, I apologize for the delay in getting back to you. I was waiting for an answer" is much more appropriate.

- DON'T USE CAPS LOCK. Typing in caps lock is generally interpreted as shouting. You might not mean it that way, but don't be surprised if people get very upset if you email them in all caps.

- Be smart. Never say anything via email that you would not say openly to others. Email is like a loaded gun, it has the ability to quickly hurt someone with just one flick of the finger. Before hitting send take a quick minute to re-read the email. Would you feel comfortable saying the things you've written out loud to the people involved? Remember, anything you write in an email can be quickly disseminated around tens, hundreds, or even thousands of people. Be smart; if you are not sure you should say it, then don't.

47) Find A Mentor

Is there someone in your office who has worked there a long time? Instead of rolling your eyes at someone who does things "the old way," try learning from them. You don't have to officially ask them to mentor you, just ask them questions. Ask them how they would handle certain situations, the best way to do something, and if possible, spend some time watching them do their job. Experience can teach you a lot of efficient ways to do your job!

These phrases can get you valuable information from more senior representatives:

- *"You've probably encountered this in the past. What would you do?"*

- *"How would you handle this situation?"*

- *"I'm struggling and I thought I would ask someone with more experience."*

- *"Can you help me out with this? I've never run across this before."*

Being mentored by senior workers is also a good way to make more veteran workers feel less threatened by newcomers. It is a great way to acknowledge their expertise and flatter them a little! The relationship you build with long-term representatives will help you along in your career. This is a great way to build allies instead of enemies.

48) Don't Rush

Customers can tell if you are rushing to get them off the phone. It makes them feel like you are annoyed they are calling or that they are interrupting something more important. Ultimately, it can leave customers with a bad impression of you and your company. Feelings like this are likely to stick with a person.

The biggest thing you can do to avoid sounding rushed is to speak at a slow or medium pace. This allows the caller to truly understand what you are saying. If you are speaking very fast it will not only be difficult for people to understand, but it also gives the impression that you are in a hurry to get off the phone.

If the customer is asking a lot of questions that you've already answered, it might be an indication that you are going too fast. When you find yourself speaking too fast, take a deep breath. Don't be afraid of a few seconds of silence. Taking a short break can allow you to regroup and help you keep your cool in a tense situation.

If you have a set number of things to discuss on each call, a checklist can be a great tool. Tick off each item as you discuss it to ensure that nothing is missed.

As always, be sure to recap the conversation (Tip #16). This is a good way to make sure you did not rush through any important details. When you rush through a call you are likely to miss vital details and recapping is a way to ensure everything is covered.

49) Don't Take it Personally

You are likely the customer's only connection to your company. They are trying to make their voice heard and you are the only one to hear it. Unfortunately, customers do not always convey their feelings in a positive manner. As a customer service professional, you are often the punching bag for disgruntled customers. If you take every snide comment or insult to heart you will give up on your job before you ever have a chance to excel at it. Not to mention the impact all this negativity will have on your life in general!

Customers are calling you because there is a problem. For every upset customer you speak with there are many more who are happy with your company. A good way to remember this is to keep a folder or file with emails or comments from happy customers. When you're feeling beaten down read these positive messages and remember how many people you have helped.

50) Send Thank You Cards

Sometimes there are situations that warrant an "old fashioned" thank you letter. This doesn't always have to be when something bad has happened. If you had a great interaction with a customer, let them know it!

There is something very special about receiving letters or cards in the mail. Face it, it's becoming rarer and rarer these days! Customers want to feel special and there is no better way than to do something for them that most other companies would not do.

Because hand-written thank you cards are so rare nowadays, customers are likely to show others. They might put it on their desk where their coworkers can see it or brag to their friends about it. Not only will they have a frequent reminder of their good experience with you, but it also provides a topic of conversation amongst coworkers or friends. Customers have a lot of options about where to send their business. Do something that sets yourself apart from the rest!

51) Let the Customer Hang Up First

When the conversation is over, wait for the customer to hang up before disconnecting the call. The customer might think of another question at the last minute. If you hang up first it makes customers feel like you are hanging up on them.

Some customers might wait for you to hang up first. If the customer is waiting for you, try one of these phrases:

- *"If there's nothing further you need from me, I am going to hang up now."*

- *"Unless there's anything else I can do, I'm going to disconnect now."*

- *"I think we've addressed all of the issues, so I'm going to hang up now."*

- *"Is there anything else I can do for you before I hang up?"*

- *"Before I hang up, have I answered all of your questions?"*

This way the customer will have one last chance to ask for your assistance. This also gives you some extra assurance that the customer is not going to call back in a few minutes with another question.

52) Smile

Even if you don't serve your customers face-to-face, don't underestimate the power of putting a smile on your face! Studies show that smiling can make you feel happy even if it is not genuine. In fact, smiling is shown to boost your mood and reduce stress even if you are faking it[1].

When you put a smile on your face you are making a decision to handle each call with a positive attitude. You might not be able to choose what the customer says or how they behave, however, you can choose to put a smile on your face and handle it as best you can. This is what sets you apart from the rest!

If you need some encouragement or reasons to smile, read through Tip #29 again for tips on having a positive attitude. Put up some visual cues in your work area to remind you to smile!

---

[1] http://www.forbes.com/sites/rogerdooley/2013/02/26/fake-smile/

Congratulations--you have made it through all 52 tips!

Hopefully you have found some helpful ways to take your customer service to the next level. Remember, giving amazing customer service is not always cut and dry. What works for you with one customer may not work with another. The longer you do this job, the more you will learn the best tools and tricks to help you deal with different kinds of customers.

Stay positive and believe in your ability to provide amazing customer service!

www.ingramcontent.com/pod-product-compliance
Lightning Source LLC
Chambersburg PA
CBHW080607180526
45168CB00007B/2817